easy UKULELE

JUST FOR FUN

CLASSIC ROCK UKULELE

12 GREAT SONGS OF THE '60S, '70S, & '80S

ARRANGED BY ANDREW DUBROCK

Produced by
Alfred Music Publishing Co., Inc.
P.O. Box 10003
Van Nuys, CA 91410-0003
alfred.com

Printed in USA.

*No part of this book shall be reproduced, arranged, adapted, recorded, publicly performed, stored in a retrieval system,
or transmitted by any means without written permission from the publisher. In order to comply with copyright laws, please apply for
such written permission and/or license by contacting the publisher at alfred.com/permissions.*

ISBN-10: 0-7390-6457-6
ISBN-13: 978-0-7390-6457-3

Cover Photos
Central image models: Katrina Hruschka and Andrew Callahan / Photographer: Brian Immke, www.adeptstudios.com
3 Cherry uke: courtesy of C. F. Martin & Co • Moon: courtesy of The Library of Congress • Gramophone: © istockphoto / Faruk Tasdemir
MP3 player: © istockphoto / tpopova • Microphone: © istockphoto / Graffizone • Handstand: © istockphoto / jhorrocks
Jumping woman: © istockphoto / Dan Wilton • Woman and radio: courtesy of The Library of Congress • Sneakers: © istockphoto / ozgurdonmaz
Background: image copyright Elise Gravel, 2009, used under license from Shutterstock.com

 Contents printed on 100% recycled paper.

FOREWORD

The ukulele craze is sweeping the world. Websites like YouTube are crowded with videos of young musicians playing both old and new music on the uke. The instrument is fun and easy to play, and that's where *Classic Rock Ukulele* comes in.

This book is designed for your total enjoyment. Each song uses the original guitar parts arranged for the ukulele. Make sure to listen to the original recordings so you know how these parts should sound before you start trying to learn them. Also, check out the many examples of excellent ukulele playing on YouTube. But most important, just have fun!

—Aaron Stang, Editor
Alfred Music Publishing Co., Inc.

CONTENTS

AFTER MIDNIGHT

Words and Music by
JOHN CALE

Moderately fast rock

1. Af - ter mid - night,_____ we gon' let it all___ hang down.
2. Af - ter mid - night,_____ we gon' shake your tam - bou -

___ down.
- rine.

After Midnight - 3 - 1

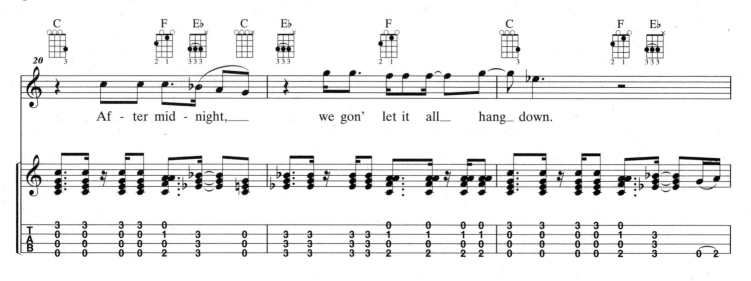

Af - ter mid - night,___ we gon' let it all__ hang_ down.

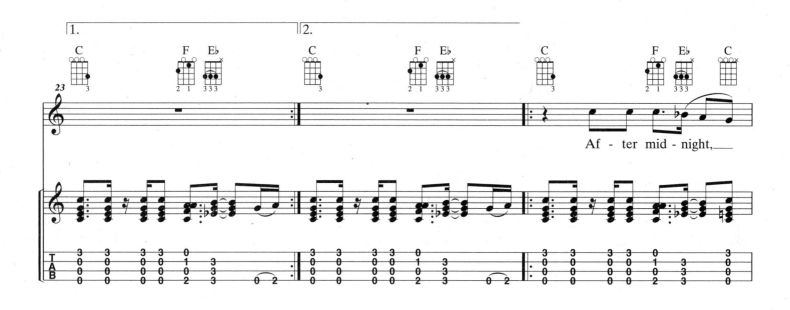

Af - ter mid - night,___

we gon' let it all__ hang__ down.

GO YOUR OWN WAY

Words and Music by
LINDSEY BUCKINGHAM

Go Your Own Way - 3 - 1

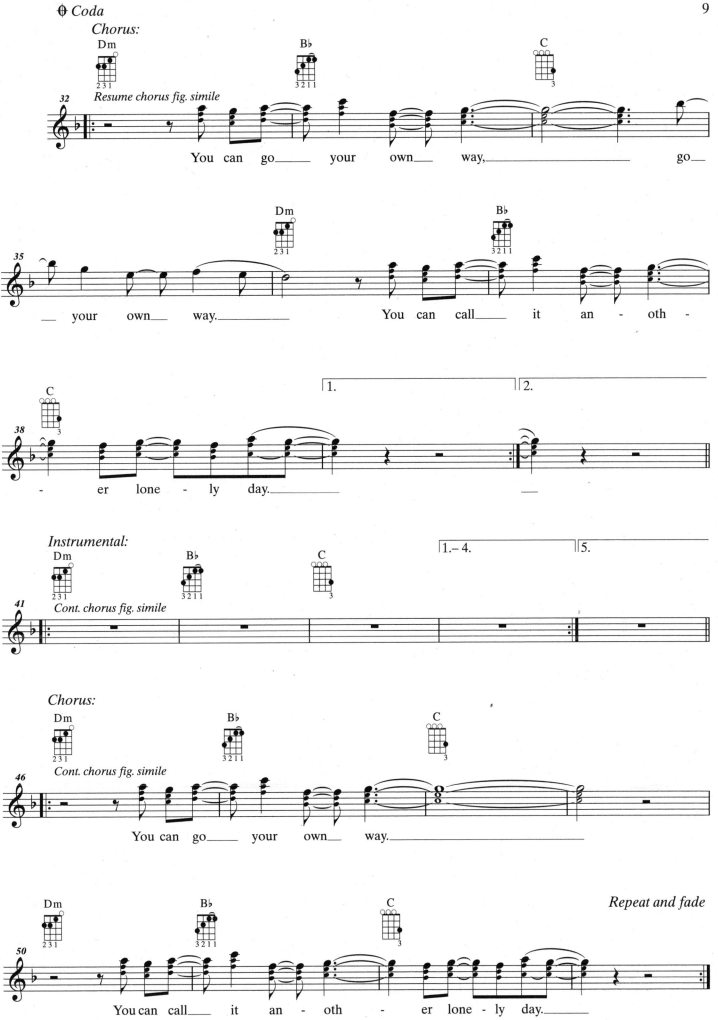

HOTEL CALIFORNIA

Words and Music by
DON HENLEY, GLENN FREY
and DON FELDER

1.On a dark des-ert high-way,_ cool_ wind in my hair,
2. Her mind is Tif-fan-y twist-ed._ She got the Mer-ce-des bends.
3. *See additional lyrics*

warm_ smell_ of co-li-tas_ ris-ing up through the air._____
She got a lot of pret-ty, pret-ty boys that she calls friends.

Up a-head in the dis-tance I saw a shim-mer-ing light.
How they dance in the court-yard, sweet sum-mer sweat.

Hotel California - 4 - 1

Repeat and fade

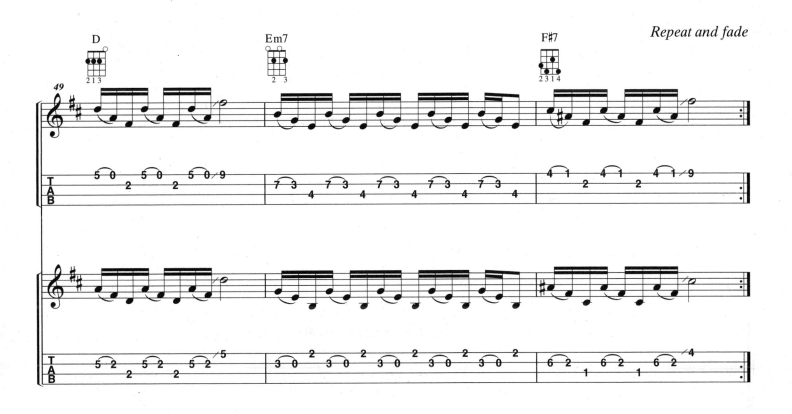

Verse 3:
Mirrors on the ceiling, the pink champagne on ice.
And she said, "We are all just prisoners here of our own device."
And in the master's chambers they gathered for the feast.
They stab it with their steely knives but they just can't kill the beast.
Last thing I remember I was running for the door.
I had to find the passage back to the place I was before.
"Relax," said the nightman, "We are programmed to receive."
You can check out anytime you like but you can never leave.

IT'S ALL OVER NOW

Words and Music by
BOBBY and SHIRLEY WOMACK

It's All Over Now - 3 - 1

16

Verse 3:
Well, I used to wake in the morning, get my breakfast in bed.
When I'd gotten worried, she'd ease my aching head.
But now she's here and there with every man in town,
Still trying to take me for that same old clown.
(To Chorus:)

It's All Over Now - 3 - 3

JUMP

Words and Music by
EDWARD VAN HALEN, ALEX VAN HALEN,
MICHAEL ANTHONY and DAVID LEE ROTH

Jump - 3 - 1

LONG TRAIN RUNNIN'

Tempo ♩ = 116

Intro:

Words and Music by
TOM JOHNSTON

* Unison G notes played on 2nd & 3rd strings.

Substitute w/Rhy. Fig. 1 *Verses 3 & 5*
Substitute w/Rhy. Fig. 2 *Verse 6*

1. Down a - round the cor - ner, half a mile from here, you
2.–6. *See additional lyrics*

see them old trains run - nin' and you watch them dis - ap - pear. With-out

Long Train Runnin' - 3 - 1

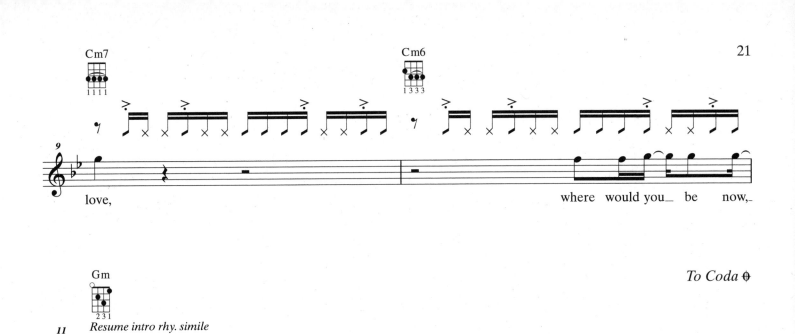

love,

where would you_ be now,_

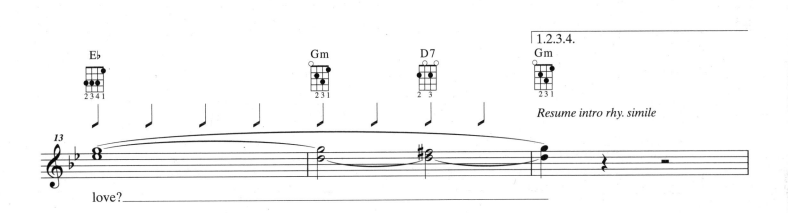

Resume intro rhy. simile

with - out

To Coda ⊕

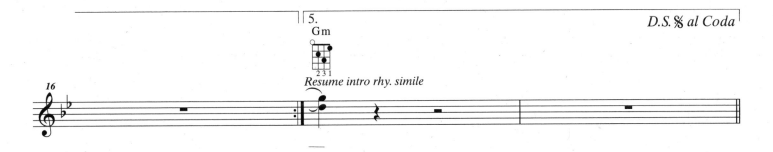

love?_____

1.2.3.4.

Resume intro rhy. simile

5.

D.S. ℅ al Coda

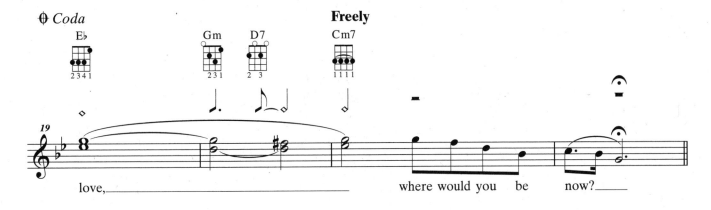

Resume intro rhy. simile

⊕ *Coda*

Freely

love,_____

where would you be now?_____

A tempo

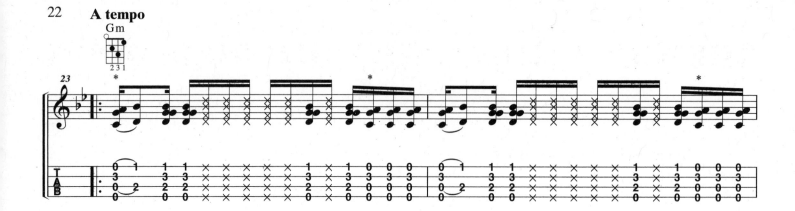

Repeat ad lib. and fade

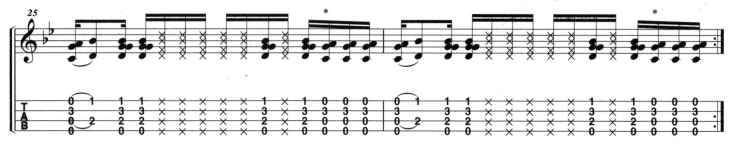

Verse 2:
You know I saw Miss Lucy,
Down along the tracks;
She lost her home and her family,
And she won't be comin' back.
Without love, where would you be right now,
Without love?

Verses 3 & 5:
Well, the Illinois Central
And the Southern Central freight,
Gotta keep on pushin', mama,
'Cause you know they're runnin' late.
Without love, where would you be right now,
Without love?
(1st time to Verse 4:)
(2nd time to Verse 6:)

Verse 4:
Instrumental Solo
(To Verse 5:)

Verse 6:
Where pistons keep on churnin'
And the wheels go 'round and 'round,
And the steel rails are cold and hard
For the miles that they go down.
Without love, where would you be right now,
Without love?
(To Coda)

THE NIGHT THEY DROVE OLD DIXIE DOWN

Words and Music by
J. ROBBIE ROBERTSON

The Night They Drove Old Dixie Down - 3 - 1

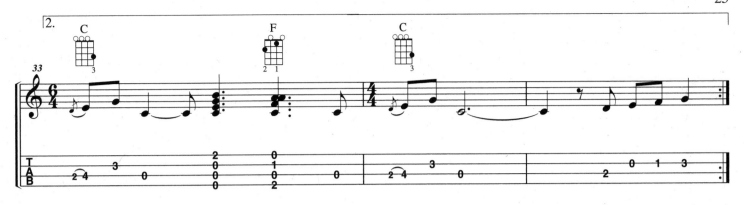

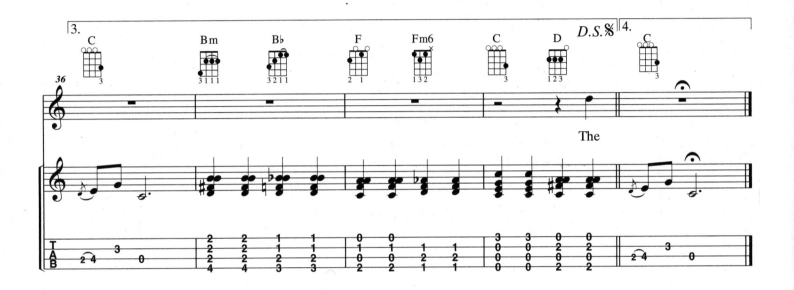

Verse 2:
Back with my wife in Tennessee,
One day she called to me,
"Virgil, quick come see,
There goes the Robert E. Lee."
Now, I don't mind choppin' wood,
And I don't care if the money's no good.
You take what you need and you leave the rest
But they should never have taken the very best.
(To Chorus:)

Verse 3:
Like my father before me,
I will work the land.
And like my brother above me,
Who took a rebel stand;
He was just eighteen, proud and brave,
But a Yankee laid him in his grave.
I swear by the mud below my feet,
You can't raise a Caine back up when he's in defeat.
(To Chorus:)

MAGGIE MAY

Words and Music by
ROD STEWART and
MARTIN QUITTENTON

Moderately ♩ = 130

Intro:

1. Wake up, Mag-gie, I___ think I got some-thing to say to you.___ It's

2.3.4. *See additional lyrics*

late Sep-tem-ber and I real-ly should_ be back___ at___ school.   I

know I keep you a-mused,___ but I feel I'm be-ing used.___   Oh,

Cont. in slashes

Cont. rhy. simile

Maggie May - 4 - 1

*D/F♯ 2nd and 3rd time only.

Mag-gie, I could-n't have tried__ an-y-more.____ You led me a-way from__ home just to save you from be-ing a - lone. You stole my heart__ and that's__ what real - ly hurts.__

2. The

Guitar Solo 1:

D.S. % al Coda

Coda   *Guitar Solo 2:*

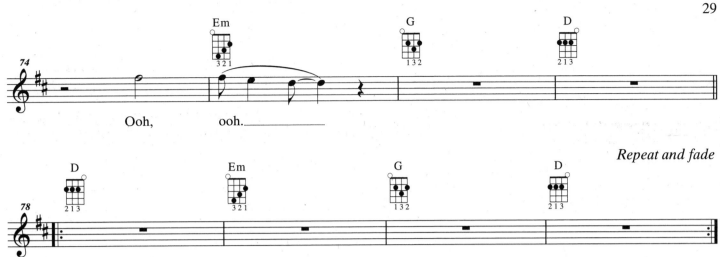

Ooh, ooh._____

Repeat and fade

Verse 2:
The morning sun, when it's in your face,
Really shows your age.
But that don't worry me none,
In my eyes you're everything.
I laughed at all of your jokes,
My love you didn't need to coax.
Oh, Maggie, I couldn't have tried anymore.
You lead me away from home
Just to save you from being alone.
You stole my soul and that's a
Pain I can do without.

Verse 3:
All I needed was a friend
To lend a guiding hand.
But you turned into a lover and, mother,
What a lover, you wore me out.
All you did was wreck my bed,
And in the morning kick me in the head.
Oh, Maggie, I couldn't have tried anymore.
You lead me away from home
'Cause you didn't want to be alone.
You stole my heart,
I couldn't leave you if I tried.
(To Guitar Solo 1:)

Verse 4:
I suppose I could collect my books
And get on back to school.
Or steal my daddy's cue,
And make a living out of playing pool.
Or find myself a rock and roll band
That needs a helping hand.
Oh, Maggie, I wish I'd never seen your face.
You made a first-class fool out of me,
But I'm as blind as a fool can be.
You stole my heart
But I love you anyway.
(To Guitar Solo 2:)

Maggie May - 4 - 4

PAINT IT, BLACK

Words and Music by
MICK JAGGER and KEITH RICHARDS

Paint It, Black - 3 - 1

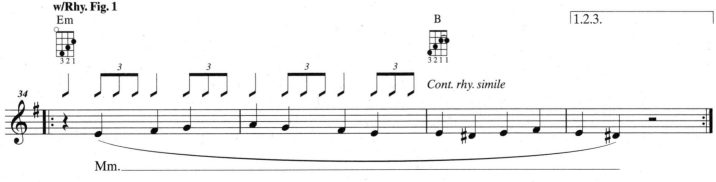

Outro:

w/Rhy. Fig. 1

Repeat and fade

Verse 3:
I look inside myself and see my heart is black.
I see my red door, I must have it painted black.

Bridge 3:
Maybe then I'll fade away and not have to face the facts.
It's not easy facing up when your whole world is black.

Verse 4:
No more will my green sea go turn a deeper blue.
I could not foresee this thing happening to you.

Bridge 4:
If I look hard enough into the setting sun,
My love will laugh with me before the mornin' comes.
(To Verse 5:)

STAIRWAY TO HEAVEN

Words and Music by
JIMMY PAGE and ROBERT PLANT

Slowly ♩ = 72

Intro:

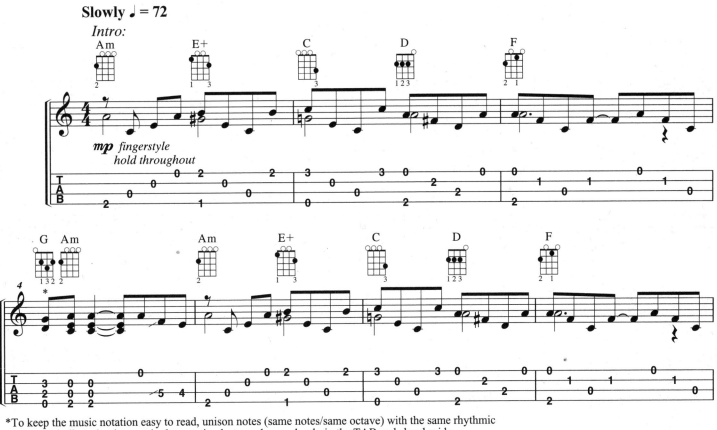

*To keep the music notation easy to read, unison notes (same notes/same octave) with the same rhythmic
value are indicated only once in the notation but are shown clearly in the TAB and chord grids.

Stairway to Heaven - 9 - 1

34

know some-times words have two mean-ings. In a tree by the brook,_ there's a

song - bird_ who sings,_ some-times all of___ our thoughts are mis - giv - en.

Interlude:

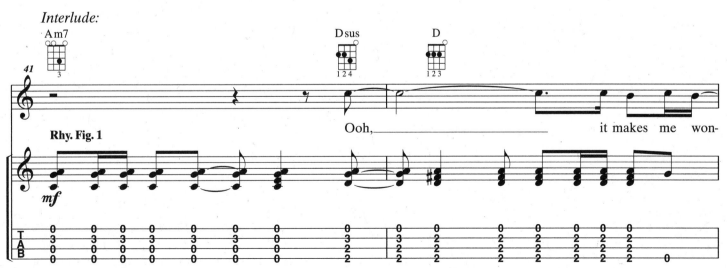

Ooh,_____ it makes me won-

Rhy. Fig. 1

Verses 4 & 5:

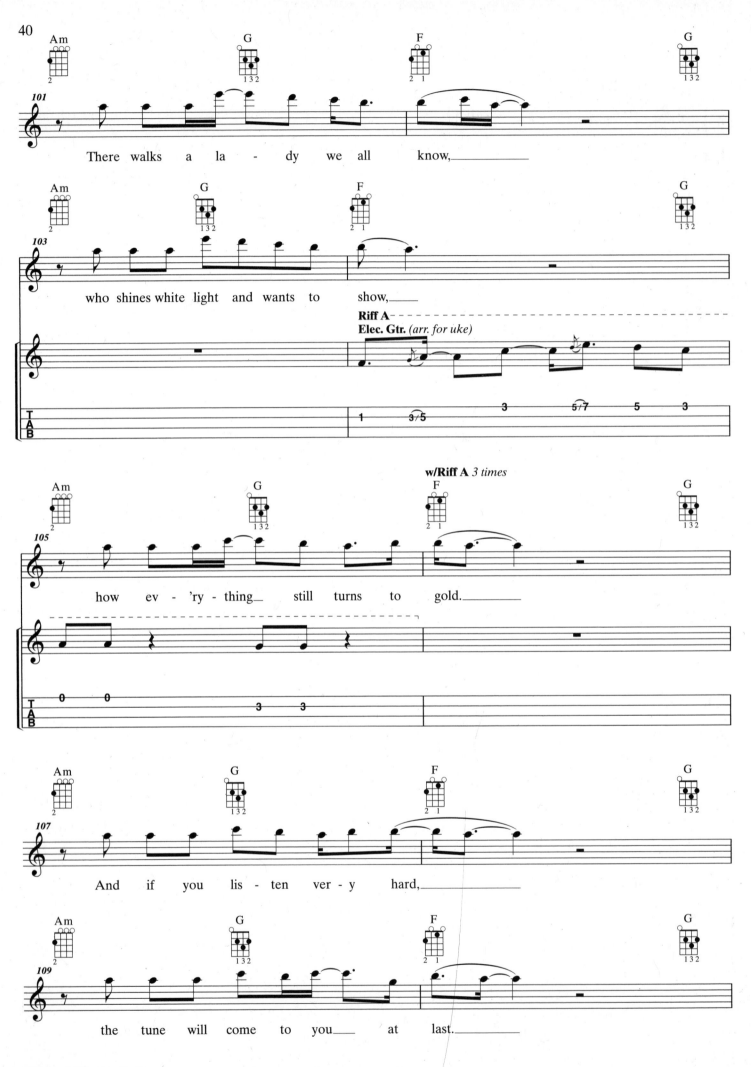

When all are one__ and one is all,_____

to be a rock__ and not to roll._____

And she's buy - ing a stair - way__ to heav - en.__

SUNSHINE OF YOUR LOVE

Words and Music by
JACK BRUCE, PETE BROWN
and ERIC CLAPTON

Moderately ♩ = 114

Intro:

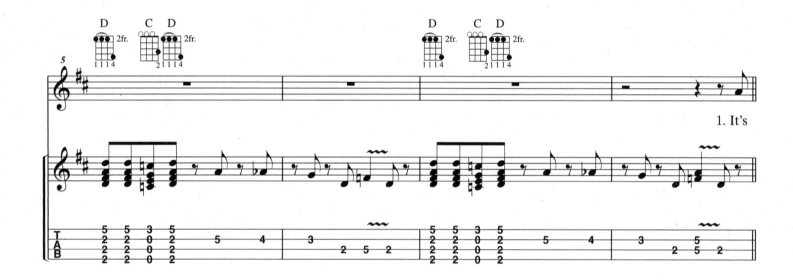

1. It's

Verse:

get-ting near dawn,____ when lights close their tired____ eyes.____
(2.4.) with you, my love,____ the light shin-ing through__ on you.____
(3.) *Guitar Solo*

Sunshine of Your Love - 4 - 1

I've_ been wait - ing so_ long, to_ be where_ I'm go - ing,

in_ the sun - shine of_ your love._

2. I'm love._

TRUCKIN'

Words by ROBERT HUNTER
Music by JERRY GARCIA,
BOB WEIR and PHIL LESH

Truckin' - 5 - 1

50

Truckin' - 5 - 5

UKULELE CHORD DICTIONARY

A CHORDS

A
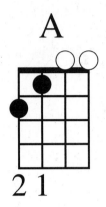
2 1

A
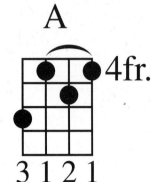
4fr.
3 1 2 1

Amaj7
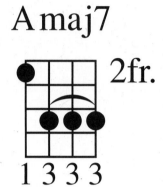
2fr.
1 3 3 3

A6
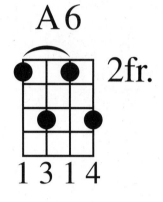
2fr.
1 3 1 4

Am
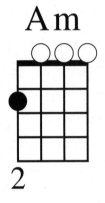
2

Am
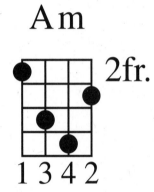
2fr.
1 3 4 2

Am7
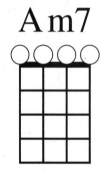

Am6
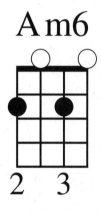
2 3

A7
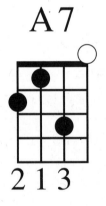
2 1 3

A7
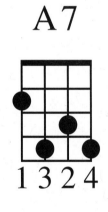
1 3 2 4

A9
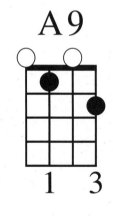
1 3

A13
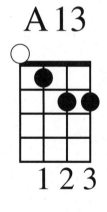
1 2 3

Asus
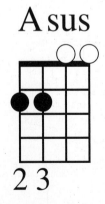
2 3

A7sus
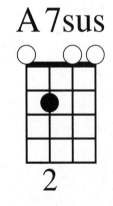
2

Adim7
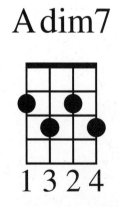
1 3 2 4

A⁺
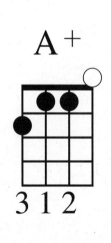
3 1 2

B♭ (A♯) CHORDS*

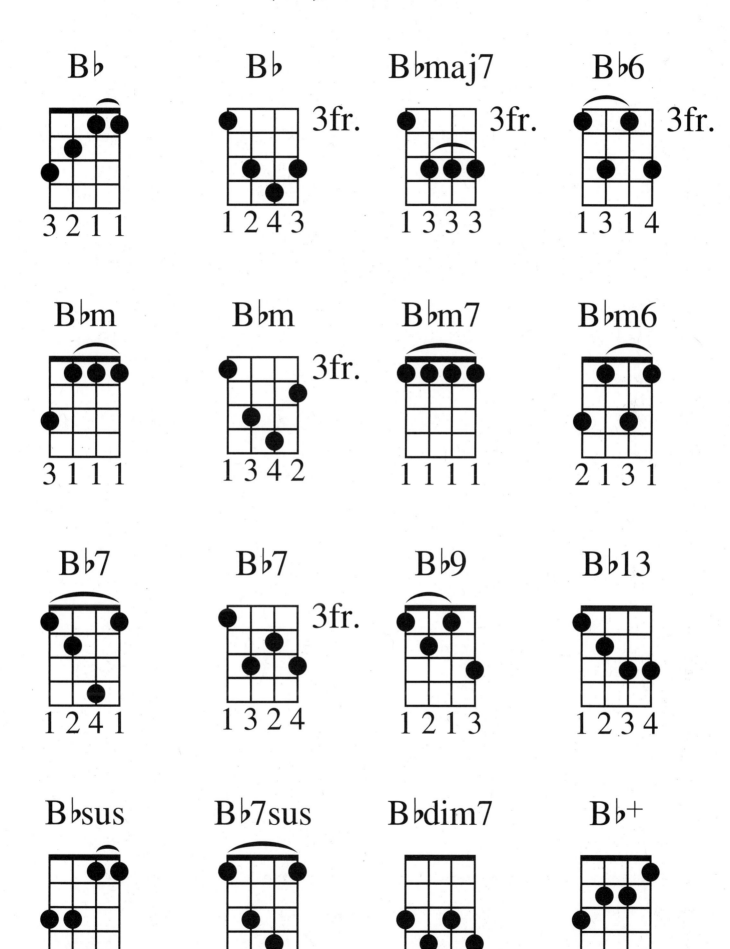

*B♭ and A♯ are two names for the same note.

B CHORDS

B
3 2 1 1

B
4fr.
1 3 4 2

B maj7
4 3 2 1

B 6
3 2 4 1

B m
3 1 1 1

B m
4fr.
1 3 4 2

B m7
1 1 1 1

B m6
2 1 3 1

B 7
3 2 1

B 7
2fr.
1 2 4 1

B 9
1 2 1 3

B 13
1 2 3 4

B sus
2 3 1 1

B 7sus
1 3 1 1

B dim7
1 3 2 4

B +
4 3 2 1

C CHORDS

C
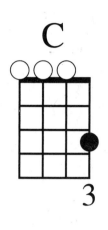
3

C
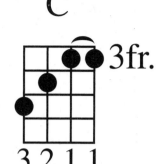
3fr.
3 2 1 1

Cmaj7
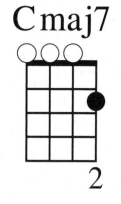
2

C6
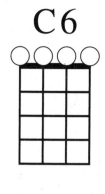

Cm
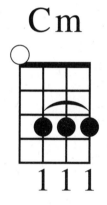
1 1 1

Cm
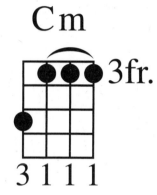
3fr.
3 1 1 1

Cm7

1 1 1 1

Cm6

1 3 3 3

C7
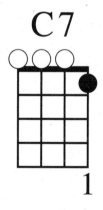
1

C7
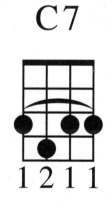
1 2 1 1

C9
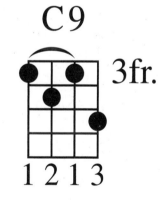
3fr.
1 2 1 3

C13
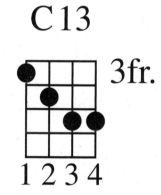
3fr.
1 2 3 4

Csus
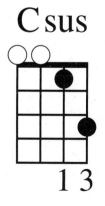
1 3

C7sus
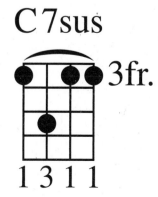
3fr.
1 3 1 1

Cdim7
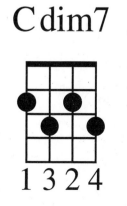
1 3 2 4

C+
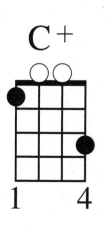
1 4

C# (D♭) CHORDS*

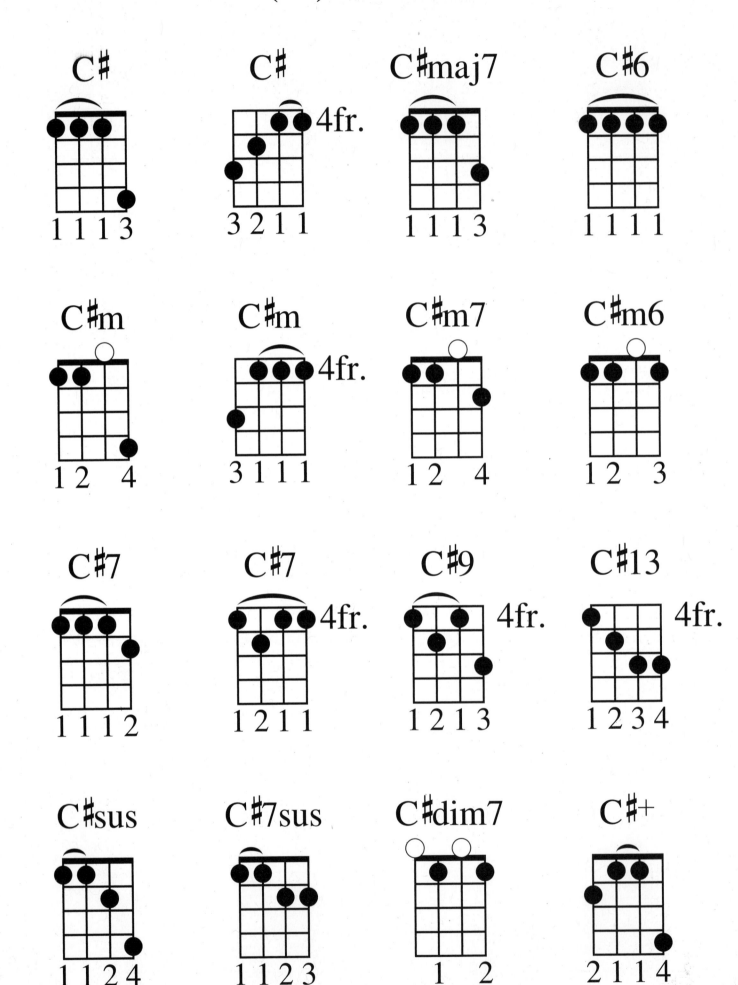

*C# and D♭ are two names for the same note.

D CHORDS

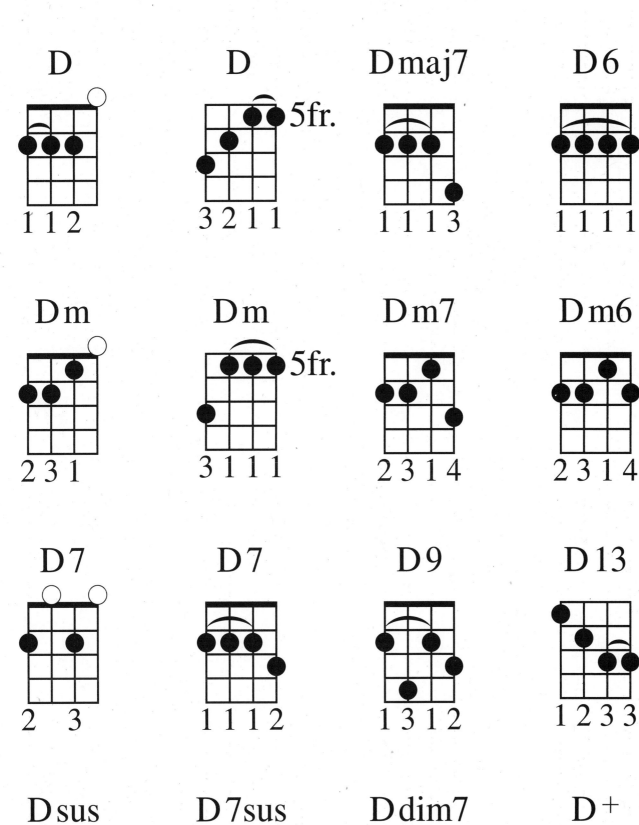

D

1 1 2

D 5fr.

3 2 1 1

Dmaj7

1 1 1 3

D6

1 1 1 1

Dm

2 3 1

Dm 5fr.

3 1 1 1

Dm7

2 3 1 4

Dm6

2 3 1 4

D7

2 3

D7

1 1 1 2

D9

1 3 1 2

D13 5fr.

1 2 3 3

Dsus 2fr.

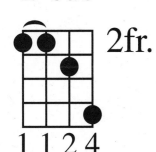

1 1 2 4

D7sus

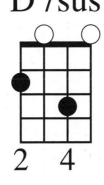

2 4

Ddim7

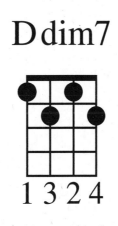

1 3 2 4

D⁺

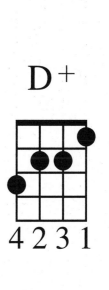

4 2 3 1

E♭ (D♯) CHORDS*

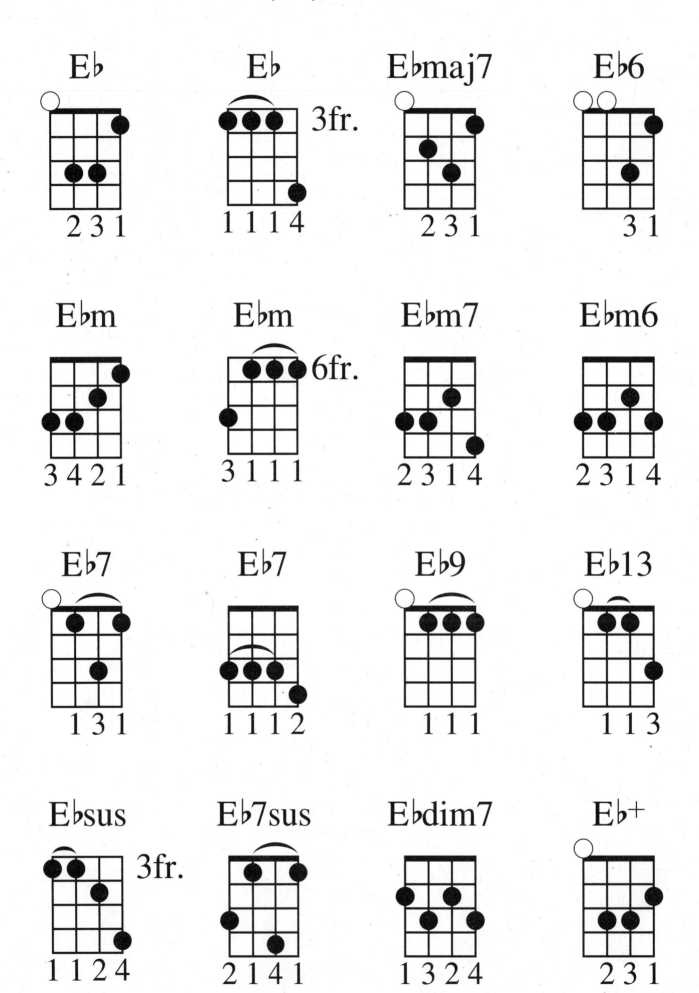

*E♭ and D♯ are two names for the same note.

E CHORDS

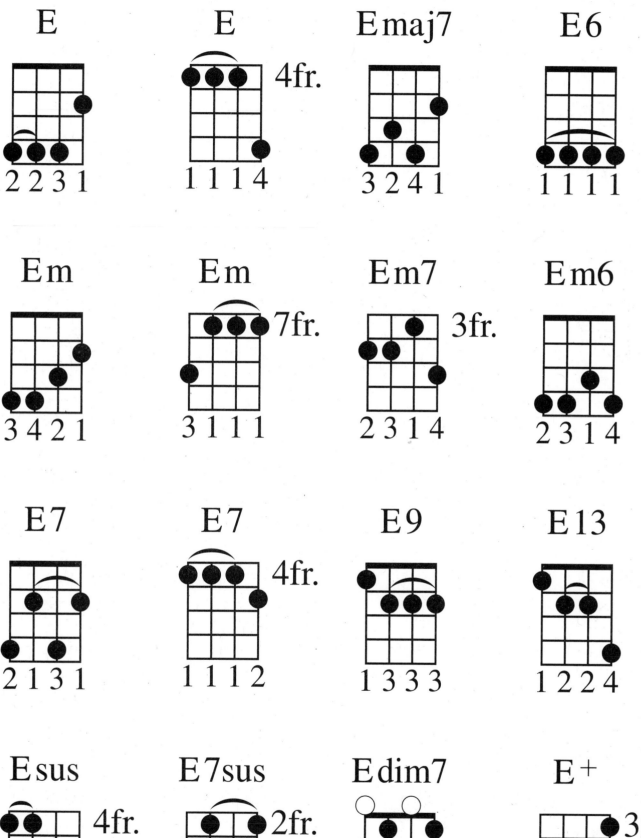

E

2 2 3 1

E 4fr.

1 1 1 4

Emaj7

3 2 4 1

E6

1 1 1 1

Em

3 4 2 1

Em 7fr.

3 1 1 1

Em7 3fr.

2 3 1 4

Em6

2 3 1 4

E7

2 1 3 1

E7 4fr.

1 1 1 2

E9

1 3 3 3

E13

1 2 2 4

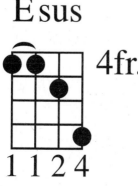

Esus 4fr.

1 1 2 4

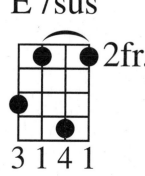

E7sus 2fr.

3 1 4 1

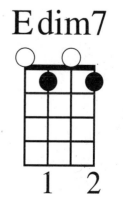

Edim7

1   2

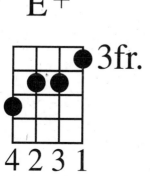

E+ 3fr.

4 2 3 1

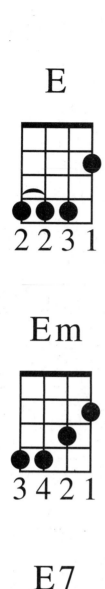

F CHORDS

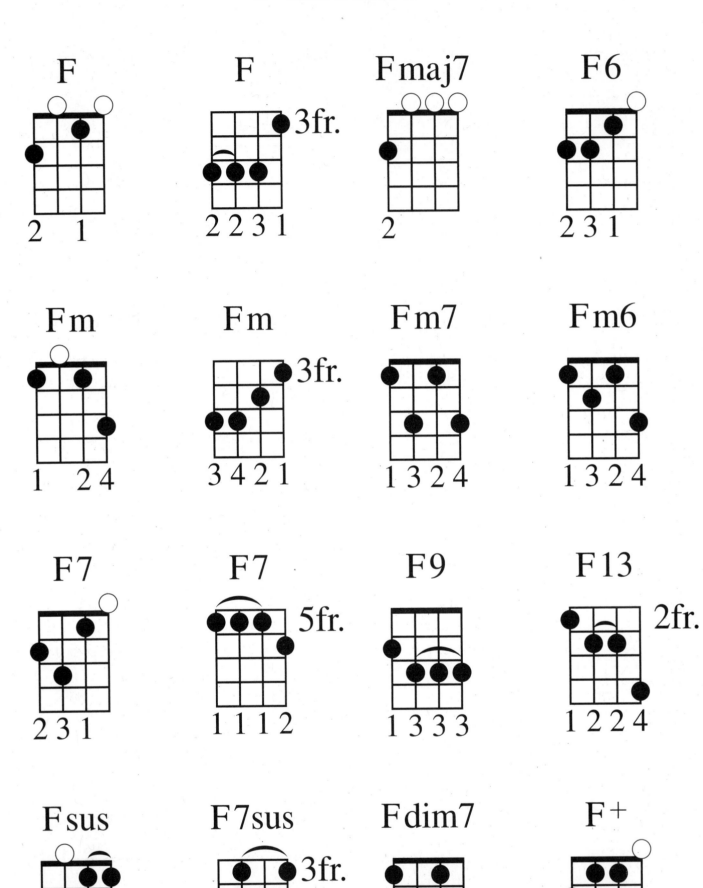

F♯ (G♭) CHORDS*

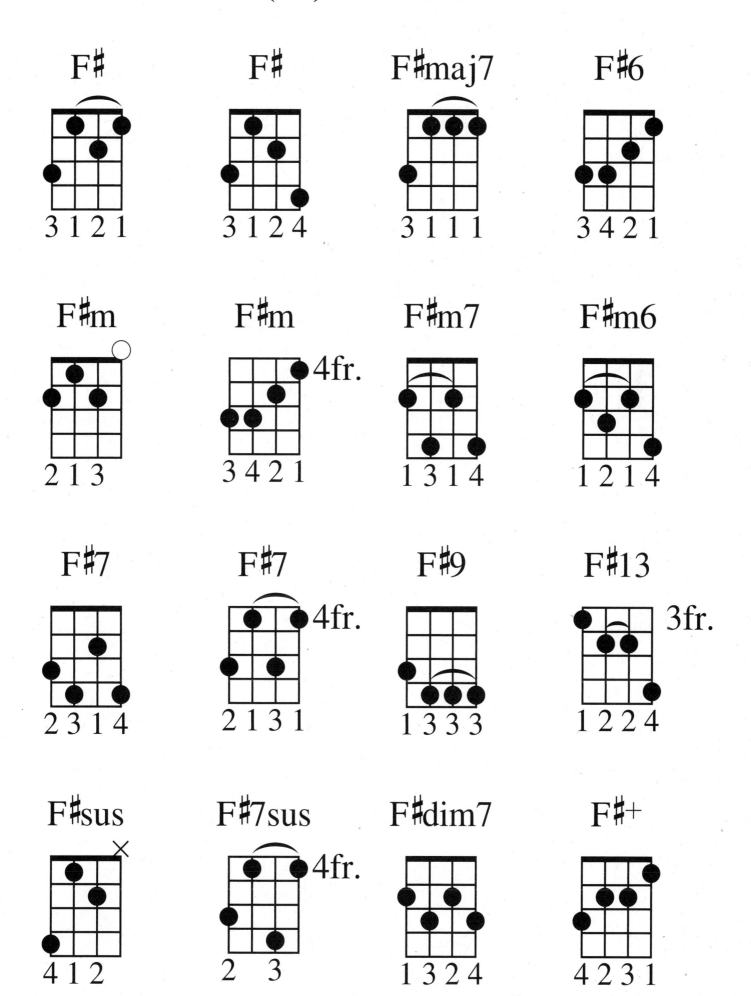

G CHORDS

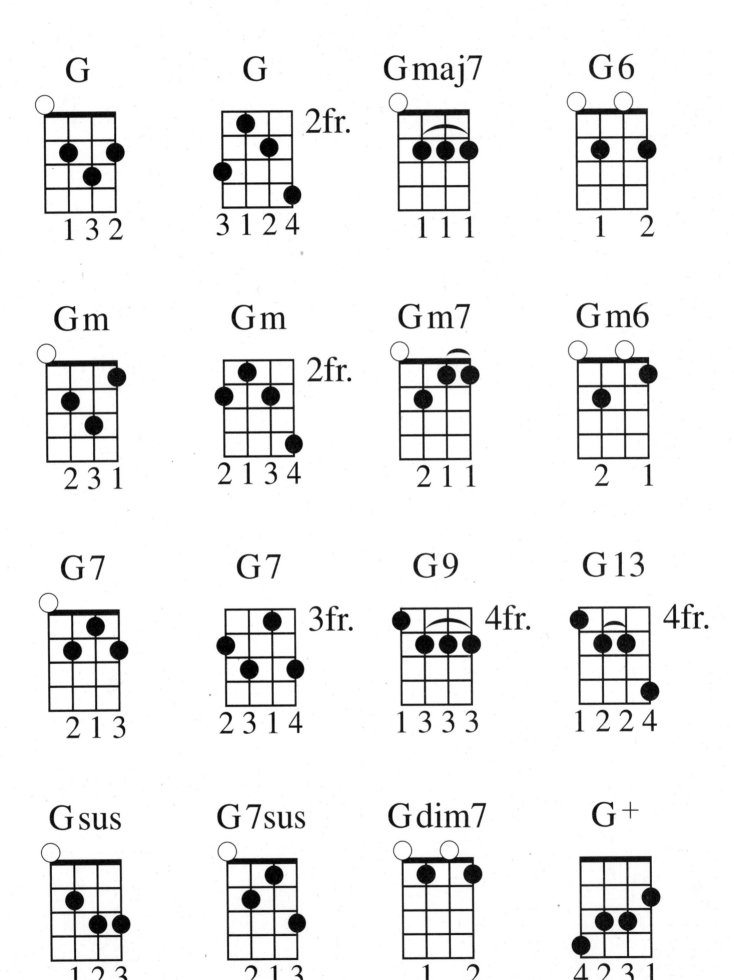

A♭ (G♯) CHORDS

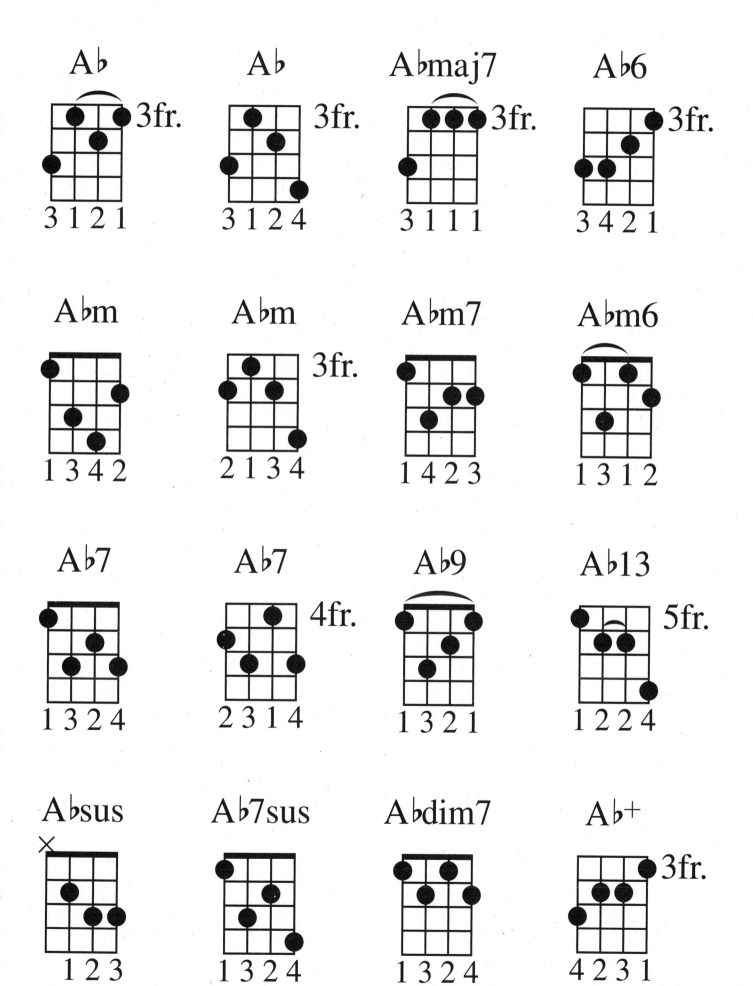

*A♭ and G♯ are two names for the same note.